How to Use This Book

This book includes four classes and a variety of activities for you to do with your child. Here are the five easy steps to having success with this book:

1. Schedule a set time each week to do one of the classes with your child (such as Sundays at 4:00 or Tuesdays at 7:30). Pick a time that consistently works for your schedule each week. There are four classes, so you will be doing one class a week for a four-week period.
2. Do the class with your child in a location with as few distractions as possible (such as outside, in a room with no one else in it, or even at your office).
3. Don't be discouraged if your child gets distracted, simply find a part of that lesson or an activity they like and spend the most time on that. Anything they can relate to is a success, even if it is only part of the lesson! If you feel part of a class is too basic or too advanced for your child, simply skip it. There are plenty of other ideas at the end of the class and in the activities section to substitute.
4. Feel free to add your own flair and ideas to each lesson, and ask questions of your child that relate to your family and life.
5. Most of all just enjoy the set time each week with your child that you do your class and have fun!

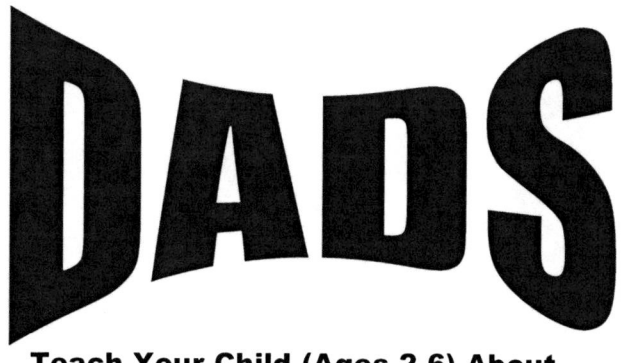

Teach Your Child (Ages 2-6) About

Being Green

By,

Bobbi Ireland

www.WonderDads.com

Robinson Public Library District
606 North Jefferson Street
Robinson, IL 62454-2699

Copyright © 2008 by WonderDads Inc.

All rights reserved. Printed in the United States of America.

No part of this publication may be reproduced or distributed in any form or by any means, or stored in a database or retrieval system, except as permitted under Sections 107 or 108 of the U.S. Copyright Act, without prior written permission of the publisher. This book is printed on acid-free paper.

Material in this book should only be done with adult supervision. WonderDads encourages parents to not engage in any activities they feel could be harmful to their child or that their child may try to do again without an adult presence. Because this book is intended for children ages 2-6, there may be some activities which are more suited for children closer to age 6. WonderDads assumes no liability for any direct or indirect injuries that occur when using this book.

WonderDads books may be purchased for educational and promotional use. For information, please e-mail store@wonderdads.com or visit us at www.WonderDads.com.

ISBN: 978-1-935153-05-4

For corrections, updates, comments, or any other inquiries, please e-mail info@wonderdads.com.

First Printing, 2008
10 9 8 7 6 5 4 3 2 1

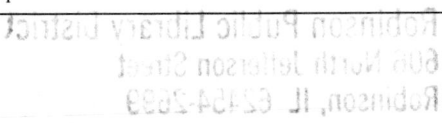

About WonderDads

Make the Time. Be a Hero.

www.WonderDads.com

WonderDads is committed to providing Dads with dynamic parenting books, do-it-yourself classes, and other products for Dads and kids that make learning more fun. Founded by a Dad who was frustrated by the lack of books and classes geared towards Dads (and class times during the day when he could not escape from work), WonderDads products are an excellent way for Dads to have consistent quality time with their child in a more dad-friendly format. We feel so lucky to be able to create products that enable Dads to form a special bond with their kids while learning about a specific topic! WonderDads is based in Maine with happy customers around the world.

Interested in Becoming a Part-Time Consultant or Author for WonderDads?

If you are interested in becoming a part-time consultant with WonderDads, please email info@wonderdads.com. We are consistently looking for (see text from website) and say that they get a commission on sales from stores they set up.

If you are interested in writing a book or have a product idea for WonderDads, please email info@wonderdads.com with information on your background, the idea, why you are qualified on this idea and any resources you would have to help market/distribute the book/product.

Dads, Teach Your Child About Being Green

Table of Contents

Class 1 – Conserving Water	Page 9
Class 2 – Composting	Page 19
Class 3 – Recycling	Page 27
Class 4 – Eating Greener & More	Page 37
Ideas for Additional Activities	Page 45
Vocabulary	Page 67
Web Sites	Page 75
Notes on the Experience With Your Child	Page 77
Write a Letter to Your Child for 20 Years From Now	Page 81
Keepsakes From the Class	Page 85

Class 1

Conserving Water

*Items to Have Prepared Before
Starting the Class:*
(Approximate Prep Time – 5-10 minutes)

1. A dollar bill
2. A piece of paper that says, "The _____ (insert name) family is going green!"
3. Index cards with written reminders to turn off the water, have some blank cards available
4. A container to set outside, and watering can
5. A cup with drinking water
6. A drawing or picture showing the water cycle
7. An idea for a 3-minute story about conserving water or a computer with Internet access to show them something on the Internet relating to conserving water
8. Read through today's lesson plan and write down any notes you might need.

How and Why Should We Conserve Water?
(Approximately 7-10 Minutes)

We use water everyday. We brush our teeth, wash our hands, take a bath or shower all with water.

Today we are going to learn about why we should conserve or save our water.

We are also going to learn how we can help our Earth by saving water.

Let's start with why we should not waste our water.

When we don't use as much water, we are helping all the animals on the Earth. If we don't use as much water, then there is more water for fish and for animals to drink.

> Question: Can you think of an animal that needs water to drink?
>
> Question: If we don't use as much water, who gets more water?

When we use less water, we save money and energy. Every time water goes down our drain, it goes to a treatment plant. It takes energy to make that water clean again. If we don't put as much water down our drains, we don't use as much energy in the water plants.

> Visual: Show your child a dollar bill.

By having more money, we can buy things we need.

> Question: Do you have any questions about why we should save water?

When we save water and help the Earth we are being "green." Isn't that a funny name?

> Visual: Show a piece of paper with the words, "The _____ family is going green!"
>
> Activity: Pick a place, together, where you can hang the sign. Then, think of ways you can save water at home. Make a list together such as: take

> shorter showers, water the lawn or flowers in the morning, collect rain water to water plants, and don't leave the water running.

Okay, we have made a great list of ways we can be green by saving water. Let's pick a place to hang up our list.

> Activity: Let's go around the house and find all the places we can get water. I have some reminder cards to place by the sinks. These cards will help us to remember to turn off the water while we are brushing our teeth. We really only need the get our toothbrush wet and then turn off the water. We can turn the water on again, to rinse off our toothbrush and to get a drink. I also have some blank cards. You can write a reminder too, if you want to.
>
> Question: Do you remember ways we can save water?

Play Time/Role Play/Drawing Time/Dress-Up
(Approximately 7-10 minutes)

Encourage your child to pretend he/she is taking a shower. Since it is only pretend, he/she can stand in the shower with clothes on. You don't actually turn on the water.

1. Set a timer for 3-5 minutes.
2. Next, explain to your child that you will be brushing your teeth and he/she will need to tell you what you are doing wrong.
3. Put toothpaste on your toothbrush, turn on the water and leave it running while you brush.
4. Your child should recognize that you should have turned off the water while you brushed.
5. Then, have your child brush his/her teeth.

An alternative idea is to take a bowl outside to be used as a "rain catcher." Then, your child gets to be the "rain" and fill up the bowl with a watering can. Say things like "It's raining; it's raining, in our rain catcher."

Then pretend to notice how the rain has filled up the bowl. Let your child use the "rain" in the bowl to water plants.

Explain that this time, you made it rain. But next time the bowl would fill up naturally by the real rain.

An alternative idea is to draw a chart about saving water. Put your names on the chart and list how you are going to save water. Each time you or your child does the task that saved water, you can put a sticker on the chart.

Why We Should Save Water
(Approximately 5 minutes)

Now let's talk about our water. Our Earth has more water than land. Did you know that there are two types of water? We have salt water and fresh water on our Earth. Most of the water on Earth is salt water. We can't drink salt water.

> Question: What are the two types of water on Earth?
>
> Visual: Give your child a cup with drinking water. Have him/her take a drink.

Did you know that the water you just drank could have been the same water that a dinosaur drank? The Earth recycles our water all the time. When it rains or snows water falls to the ground and into oceans and streams. When it stops raining, some of the water evaporates and floats back up into the air and creates clouds. After awhile, it rains or snows again and the water is back on land and in oceans, and streams. Then it does it again. Our water is always going up, down, and back up again.

> Visual: Show a picture or drawing of a cloud with rain coming down to land. Show arrows going down from the cloud to the ground and then another arrow pointing up from the ground. This is called the water cycle.
>
> Question: Do you have any questions about the water cycle?
>
> Activity: Let's pretend we are the water cycle. First let's be the rain falling from the sky. Now, we are a puddle of rain on our driveway. The sun is coming out and it is getting really warm. We are starting to

evaporate. Let's go back up into the air. Look, I am a cloud, I am getting really big. I'm floating around in the sky. Now, I am getting really full with water. It's time to rain again. I'm rain, falling to the earth. But this time, I landed at the _____ (pick a place, it could any fun place your child likes to go).

Story Time/Internet Time
(Approximately 5-10 minutes)

Read your child a story that tells about saving water. You can check your local library and the Internet. Some stories may be found online. Some children's books that are available are:

Saving Water (First Facts: Water All Around) by: Rebecca Olien

Saving Water (Green Kinds) by: Neil Morris, Amanda Askew, and Wendy Horobin

The Water Cycle by: Trudi Strain Trueit.

The following Internet sites have online games all about saving water:

http://www.epa.gov/watersense/kids/games.htm

http://www.dinosaurdesign.com/LeakyGame.htm

http://www.savingwater.org/kids/k-3_games.htm

13

Review for Today's Lesson
(Approximately 2 minutes)

Let's go over what we learned in our class today.

Do you remember why we should save water?

By saving water, what kinds of animals get more water to drink?

What are some ways we can save water at home?

What happens to the rain or snow after it falls on land or in the oceans?

What can we do with rain water that we collect?

What was your favorite part about our class today?

Do you have any final questions?

If You Have Extra Time

Review Vocabulary Section in this book.
Review Websites Section in this book.
Review Additional Activities Section in this book.
Take a picture with yourself and your child holding any items that were relevant with today's class.
Spend more time telling stories.
Share a snack and talk about today's class.

Dad's Notes from Today's Class
(Such as what your child found most interesting, what to touch on again, and other ideas on the topic. Focus on these again in the next class.)

Order a Framed Certificate of Completion for Your Child to Hang on Their Wall

Order now so that you can give it to your child when you complete the last class.

The certificate includes a space to write in your name, your child's name and the title of the class. The full-color certificate is in a frame ready for hanging in your child's room. A great keepsake for years to come!

To Order, Visit
www.WonderDads.com/merchandise3.asp

Class 2

Composting

*Items to Have Prepared Before
Starting the Class:*
(Approximate Prep Time – 5-10 Minutes)

1. Small container of soil
2. Picture of a landfill (can be found on the Internet)
3. Make a list of products that can be composted. If possible add pictures for a better visual.
4. Wire flags (optional)
5. Picture of a compost pile (can be found on the Internet)
6. Bag or box to collect a few items in
7. Picture of a worm compost system, or vermiculture (can be found on the Internet)
8. An idea for a 3-minute story about conserving water or a computer with Internet access to show them something relating to conserving water
9. Read through today's lesson plan and write down any notes you might need.

How and Why Should We Compost?
(Approximately 7-10 minutes)

When we grow fruits, vegetables, and flowers we dig a hole and plant a seed. But do you know what is in the soil?

> Visual: Show your child soil.

The soil has recycled all of the old plants that have died. The more nutrients or food the soil has, the richer the soil is and the better things will grow.

We can help to feed our soil by giving it our scraps to eat. The soil will break down the scraps and we will have created a compost pile. Then, when good, rich soil is needed, we can use our compost.

Right now, when we are done with vegetable scraps, natural products, leaves, and grass scraps, we throw them away. Our wastes become part of landfills, or dumps.

> Visual: Show a picture of a landfill.
>
> Question: What will happen to the landfills if people keep throwing away waste?

Here are some items that can be put in a compost pile instead of being thrown in the trash.

> Visual: Show your child the paper with pictures of items that can be composted.
>
> Activity: Pick a spot in the yard to create a compost pile. Choose a level, well drained area. It is best to pick a spot that won't be the main attraction of your yard. Keep in mind that your compost pile will look like a mound of materials. Make sure your area is directly on the ground. You will want the worms to be able to help in the compost pile. To help our child see the new area, you can place a few wire flags around the area.

Once we have a compost pile, we will be able to use that organic material for flower beds and anywhere in the yard. Our flowers and plants will be prettier and healthier

Now that we have an area for our compost pile, let's go inside and see if we have any materials that can we can "feed" it.

> Activity: Look around your house for the following materials: paper napkins, freezer burnt fruit, lint from the dryer, coffee grounds, coffee filters, fruit peelings, egg shells (not eggs), stale bread, and newspaper. If you use newspaper, napkins, or coffee filters, tear them up in pieces. Collect all the items in a bag or box.

We can always "feed" our compost grass, leaves, and kitchen scraps, but we can never feed it meat or dairy products. We can also water our compost pile. We want to keep it moist.

When looking for things to compost, try to find things that are green and brown. These two colors keep a balance. Never put weeds in your compost pile. Weeds can grow anywhere and we don't want a weedy compost pile.

> Visual: Show your child a picture of a compost pile.
>
> Question: Do you have any questions about why we should compost our waste?

We call making compost "going green." The _____ (insert name) family is going green!

Play Time/Role Play/Drawing Time/Dress-Up
(Approximately 5 minutes)

Play the Treasure Hunt game.
1. Go around the house looking for items to compost. The first person to find five new compost items wins.
2. Take turns doing a role play. Pretend to be "Wesley or Wanda Waster." They don't think composting is necessary and they throw everything away.

3. The other person catches "Wesley or Wanda" throwing away items that could be composted.

An alternative idea is to have them draw a picture of a compost pile and a garden of beautiful flowers beside the compost pile.

Ways We Can Compost
(Approximately 7-10 minutes)

We talked about why we should compost our waste materials and we picked a spot to compost in our yard. Each time we compost it is helping our Earth and reducing the waste in landfills.

Let's talk about another way we can compost. Did you know that one of Earth's best ways to compost is with worms? It's true. Worms can compost our wastes in a quick amount of time.

> Visual: Show a picture of a vermiculture, a worm compost system.

Not everyone has a backyard suitable for a compost pile. Many people have chosen to create a compost system with worms. People can buy these systems or they can be made.

> Question: Would you ever like to have a worm compost system?

The compost material from the worms is a very rich and natural soil fertilizer. That means it's good for the soil.

> Question: If we had a worm compost system and we had compost material from it, where could we use that organic material?

When people make a worm compost system there are certain worms to use. You don't dig the worms up from the ground. You actually need red wigglers or red earthworms. The best place to find them is at bait stores.

The red wigglers and red earthworms feel comfortable contained in the compost system. The worms from our soil are happier in the large yard.

> Activity: Let's think of items that could be put into a worm compost system.
> (Anything organic can be used.)
>
> Question: Do you have any questions about worm compost systems?
>
> Question: What are the two ways of composting that we talked about today?

Story Time/Internet Time
(Approximately 5-10 minutes)

Read a story to your child that tells about saving water. You can check your local library and the Internet. Some stories may be found online. Some children's books that are available are:

Basic Composting: All the Skills and Tools You Need to Get Started (Basic How-to Guides) by Erich Ebeling

Compost, By Gosh! by Michelle Eva Portman

Worms Eat My Garbage: How to Set Up and Maintain a Worm Composting System by Mary Appelhof.

The following Internet sites have online games all about composting:

http://www.bravekidgames.com/flash_game_home_compost.php

http://www.ciwmb.ca.gov/vermi/game/menu.html

Review of Today's Lesson
(Approximately 5 minutes)

Let's go over what we learned in our class today.

Do you remember why we should compost?

By composting what happens to our landfills?

What are some things we can compost?

What two colors do we think of when we compost?

What can we do with the organic material after it is composted?

What was your favorite part about our class today?

Do you have any final questions?

If You Have Extra Time

Review Vocabulary Section in this book.
Review Websites Section in this book.
Review Additional Activities Section in this book.
Take a picture with yourself and your child holding any items that were relevant with today's class.
Have more story time.
Share a snack and talk about today's class.

Dad's Notes from Today's Class
(Such as what your child found most interesting, what to touch on again, and other ideas on the topic. Focus on these again in the next class.)

Dads, Teach Your Child About Being Green

Class 3

Recycling

*Items to Have Prepared Before
Starting the Class:*
(Approximate Prep Time – 5-10 Minutes)

1. Two bottles of water
2. Picture of a landfill
3. Picture of the recycle triangle
4. A plastic product that has the recycle triangle on it
5. A picture showing litter
6. A few articles of clothing that you want to recycle
7. Four cardboard boxes to separate recycling products into
8. Empty plastic bottles to use as bowling pins
9. An idea for a 3-minute story about conserving water or a computer with Internet access to show them something relating to conserving water
10. Read through today's lesson plan and write down any notes you might need.

How and Why Should We Recycle?
(Approximately 7-10 minutes)

We use products everyday that come in some kind of container. Recycling means to take the product when we are done with it, and turn it into another useful product.

Today we are going to learn about why we should recycle.

We're also going to learn about how we can help the Earth by starting to recycle our own products.

Let's start with why we should recycle.

When I'm thirsty I love to drink water in a bottle.

> Visual: Show your child two small bottles of water. Give one to your child and keep one.

I am really thirsty, how about you? As we go through this class, let's drink our water and at the end of our class, maybe we will know what we should do with our empty bottles.

> Visual: Show your child the picture of the landfill from the last class.

Do you remember in our last class when we talked about landfills and composting? Not only are landfills filled with things we can compost, they are also filled with things we can't compost but we can recycle.

> Visual: Show your child a picture of the recycle arrow and what type of products can be recycled.

When we buy food or drinks at the grocery store they usually come in containers that we throw away. But a box can be turned into something else. This is also true for glass and plastic.

You may have seen a little triangle on the bottoms of products.

> Visual: Show a product that has the triangle recycle symbol on it.

Dads, Teach Your Child About Being Green

Anytime we see this symbol it means the product can be recycled. The three arrows mean collecting, processing, and creating the product into a new product.

> Question: If we recycled old products instead of throwing them away what would happen to the landfills? Are you still drinking your water?

Anytime we can recycle products it keeps them out of landfills and helps keep pollution off of the Earth and out of our air.

> Activity: Let's check in the kitchen and find products that have the recycle arrows on the bottom. (The products don't have to be empty. You will only be using them as a demonstration)

Now that we have found some items that can be recycled, let's separate them into boxes. Items that are made with the same material have to be grouped together. Let's put the glass together, the cans together, the plastic together, and the paper together.

> Activity: Can you find all of the products made with glass? Let's put them here. Now, how about the plastics? They can go here. And lastly, let's put the paper in the last box. When we really start recycling, all of the products to be recycled will have to be empty and clean. But, for today, we are just practicing with these products.

Now that we have all the products separated for recycling, we can take them to a recycling center. Sometimes trash companies have special recycling pick-ups. They will not only pick up regular trash but they will also pick up recycling products too.

> Question: What do we do with an empty product that has three arrows in the shape of a triangle?

Play Time/Role Play/Drawing Time/Dress-Up
(Approximately 7-10 minutes)

Bowling Time:
1. Set up empty plastic bottles. They can be a variety of different plastic bottles (soda, ketchup, dressing, etc.).
2. Then take turns with your child using a ball to knock down the empty plastic bottles.
3. Keep this bowling game in a box and use it another time.

An alternative idea is to have a box of recyclables. There will be a mixture of paper and plastic. See how fast you and your child can separate the paper and plastics into boxes.

Ways We Can Recycle
(Approximately 7-10 minutes)

We talked about why we should recycle used materials. Each time we recycle we are helping the Earth and helping to create something new from something old.

Not everyone recycles. Unfortunately some people actually litter. Littering is when people throw trash on the Earth instead of recycling or composting. I see litter when I am driving. Some people just throw trash out their car window.

Visual: Show a picture of litter. You can find one on the Internet.

Question: Have you ever seen litter by the road?

Litter can be as small as a chewing gum wrapper and as large as a big trash bag. Either way, it's still littering.

Question: If everyone threw out just one piece of litter, what would the Earth look like?

We can do our part by not littering. Many communities offer "clean up" programs where volunteers help pick up litter.

Another way we can do our part in recycling is to recycle our old clothes and toys.

> Visual: Show your child a few old clothing items that you no longer want.

I don't wear these clothes anymore, but instead of throwing them into the trash, I will take them to a place that collects old clothes.

> Activity: Let's look in my room and your room and find more clothes and maybe some toys that we don't want anymore. Then, we will take them to the clothing collection center and someone else will be very happy when they find these.

Story Time/Internet Time
(Approximately 5-10 minutes)

Read your child a story that tells about recycling. You can check your local library and the Internet. Some stories may be found online. Some children's books that are available are:

Why Should I Recycle? (Why Should I?) by Jen Green and Mike Gordon

Recycle!: A Handbook for Kids by Gail Gibbons

The Three R's: Reuse, Reduce, Recycle (What Do You Know About? Books) by Nuria Roca and Rosa M. Curto

The following Internet sites have online games all about recycling:

http://resources.kaboose.com/games/michael recycle.html?source=gamesInv&kw=michaelmichaelLN

http://www.recyclezone.org.uk/home_fz.aspx

http://www.squiglysplayhouse.com/Games/Flash/PuzzleStrategy/Recycle/index.php

Review for Today's Lesson
(Approximately 2 Minutes)

Let's go over what we learned in our class today.

Do you remember why we should recycle?

By recycling what happens to our landfills?

What is littering?

What are some products we can recycle?

Can we recycle clothing and toys?

What was your favorite part about our class today?

Do you have any final questions?

Activity: Remember our bottles of water we were drinking during this class? Is your bottle empty? What do you think we should do with our empty water bottles?

If You Have Extra Time

Review Vocabulary Section in this book.
Review Websites Section in this book.
Review Additional Activities Section in this book.
Take a picture with yourself and your child holding any items that were relevant with today's class.
Have more story time.
Share a snack and talk about today's class.

Dad's Notes from Today's Class

(Such as what your child found most interesting, what to touch on again, and other ideas on the topic. Focus on these again in the next class.)

Don't Make the Next Class the Last One with Your Child

Order Another Book Today:

Dads, Teach Your Child About:

Football   Baseball   The Computer   Being Green   Rock & Roll   What Daddy Does as a Businessman   What Daddy Does as a Lawyer   What Daddy Does as a Doctor   Safety Lessons   Manners   Being Catholic   Being Jewish   Becoming a Brother   Becoming a Sister   How to Do a Magic Trick   How to Bake

& Many More Titles…

www.WonderDads.com

Class 4

Eating Greener & More

*Items to Have Prepared Before
Starting the Class:*
(Approximate Prep Time – 5-10 Minutes)

1. Picture of a farmer's market
2. Package of carrots
3. Carrots without packaging
4. Paper, pen/pencil
5. Paper, markers/crayons
6. Organic strawberries, organic vanilla yogurt, bowl
7. An idea for a 3-minute story about conserving water or a computer with Internet access to demonstrate something relating to organic food
8. Read through today's lesson plan and write down any notes you might need.

How Can We Eat Greener?
(Approximately 7-10 minutes)

We have been talking about different ways we can become green. Today, we are going to learn how we can eat greener. I'm not talking about eating more foods that are green in color.

I'm talking about eating foods that are organic. Organic foods are grown on farms that don't use chemicals to help them grow. They also haven't been sprayed with dangerous pesticides. Pesticides keep bugs from eating the fruits and vegetables. The farmers use safe products to keep the bugs away. Those products aren't harmful to people or other animals.

When we eat organic fruits and vegetables, not only are we putting healthier food in our bodies, but we are also helping the Earth. When farmers don't use chemicals on their produce, the air, water and food is cleaner in that area.

Question: What if all the produce that is grown and sent to grocery stores was grown organic? What would happen to our air, water, and food?

Organic produce can include vegetables, fruits, grains, juice, dairy, eggs, and meat. Some organic foods are easier to find than others. Organic foods can be found in a grocery store. Look for the seal from the USDA that labels the food "organic." Another place to find organic produce is a farmer's market.

Visual: Show your child a picture of a farmer's market.

Buying food from a farmer's market is a way to be green. Buying from local people helps communities and is also "green."

Visual: Show a picture of a package of carrots that can be bought from the store.

When we buy vegetables from the store, they come in packages. Once we use the vegetables, we have to throw away the packaging, unless we can recycle it.

Dads, Teach Your Child About Being Green

When we buy from a farmer's market, we do not have any packaging. It comes just like this.

> Visual: Show your child an actual carrot without packaging.
>
> Activity: Let's make a list of all the products we will look for at the farmer's market. We can use this pen and paper.

When we go to the grocery store we can bring our own fabric bags. By doing that, we won't have to use their plastic bags. This helps the environment.

When we go to the grocery store we can be a little picky about the products we buy. Instead of choosing food products that have a lot of packaging, we can choose products with less packaging.

Another way to eat greener is to grow some of our own food. We can have a garden and grow vegetables. We won't use chemicals or pesticides in our garden so all of the produce will be organic.

Organic vegetables can be eaten raw. In fact, some nutrients are lost when a vegetable is cooked. Eating raw vegetables are healthier and we don't use energy to prepare them. We save energy by eating raw vegetables.

Question: What would you like to grow in a garden?

When people grow their own vegetables, they don't have to drive to the store to buy them. This cuts down on air pollution.

> Activity: Let's make a list of all the vegetables that we would like to grow in a garden using this pen and paper.

Play Time/Role Play/Drawing Time/Dress-Up
(Approximately 7-10 minutes)

Give your child a piece of paper and crayons or markers. Have your child draw a picture of his/her garden.

> Activity: You and your child take turns selling fruits and vegetables at a farmer's market. You can use real produce or pretend. One of you can be the seller and the other the buyer. Ask questions about the class to encourage comprehension of the lesson.

How Can We Eat Greener?
(Approximately 7-10 minutes)

We talked about how we can eat greener and how eating greener helps the earth. We've also talked about buying organic fruits and vegetables from farmer's markets and growing our own produce in a garden.

> Question: Do you like to have a snack after you have had a day of playing?

A good healthy snack is organic cheese sticks and an apple. Another healthy snack is a banana and organic almonds.

> Question: Are you ready to make an organic snack?
>
> Activity: Mix organic strawberries with organic vanilla yogurt. Your child can pour the strawberries into a bowl. Then add the yogurt. Mix gently. Enjoy!

Story Time/Internet Time
(Approximately 5-10 minutes)

Read a story to your child that tells about organic produce. You can check your local library and the Internet. Some stories may be found online. Some children's books that are available are:

[To Buy or Not to Buy Organic: What You Need to Know to Choose the Healthiest, Safest, Most Earth-Friendly Food]() by Cindy Burke

[A Child's Organic Garden]() by Lee Fryer and Leigh Bradford

[One Good Apple: Growing Our Food for the Sake of the Earth]() by Catherine Paladino

Growing Food We Eat (Food for Good Health) by Barbara J. Patten

The following Internet sites have online games all about organic food:

http://www.organic.org/?section=kids&page=6

http://www.envirokidz.com/fun

Review for Today's Lesson
(Approximately 2 minutes)

Let's go over what we learned in our class today.

Do you remember what it means to eat greener?

When farmers grow organic produce what happens to the air, water, and food supply?

Why should we carry a fabric bag to the grocery store?

Can we grow organic produce in a garden?

What kind of market can we find organic produce?

What was your favorite part about our class today?

Do you have any final questions?

If You Have Extra Time

Review Vocabulary Section in this book
Review Websites Section in this book
Review Additional Activities Section in this book
Take a picture with yourself and your child holding any items that were relevant with today's class.
Spend more time telling stories.
Share a snack and talk about today's class.

Dad's Notes from Today's Class
(Such as what your child found most interesting, what to touch on again, and other ideas on the topic. Focus on these again in the next class.)

Activities

Ideas for Additional Activities

Saving Water with a Bottle

You can do this activity if you don't have a water-efficient toilet.

What you'll need:
1. An empty plastic water bottle with the paper label removed.

How to do it:
1. Fill up the plastic water bottle with water.
2. Open the tank on your toilet and flush the toilet.
3. As the water fills up in the tank, place your filled water bottle on the bottom of the tank. Be careful not to let the bottle interfere with any flushing hardware.

Why do it:
If a toilet is not water-efficient, gallons of water are wasted every time the toilet is flushed. The filled water bottle takes up some of the tank's volume. Therefore, there is not as much water in the tank. This saves extra water from being flushed away each time the toilet is flushed.

Notes for the Activity:

Write a Letter

What you'll need:
1. Do some research and find a product that is on the market that is not environmentally friendly. (example: bulk packaging or plastic)
2. A paper, pen envelope and stamp.

How to do it:
1. Write a nice, respectful letter with your child to the maker of the product. Explain how different packaging would help the product to become earth-friendly. Urge them to change their packaging.

Why do it:
If people don't contact companies about their packaging then they won't change the way their product is packaged. It is a good idea for customers to express their concerns in a respectful manner. If enough people express concerns, packaging may change.

Notes for the Activity:

Container Garden #1

What you'll need:
2. An old shoe or boot that you or your child no longer wears
3. Potting soil
4. Seeds or plants

How to do it:
1. Put a few small rocks in the bottom of the shoe for drainage.
2. Put potting soil in the shoe.
3. Add the seeds or plant.
4. Water daily.

Why do it:
This is an easy project to do with your child. It is a fun way to recycle an old shoe or boot.

Notes for the Activity:

Herb and Vegetable Garden

What you'll need:
1. A place outside to plant a garden.
2. Seeds or plants of tomatoes, basil, chives, carrots, cucumbers, and oregano.

How to do it:
1. Prepare your garden for planting.
2. Plant the tomatoes beside the basil.
3. Plant the chives beside the carrots.
4. Plant the cucumbers beside the oregano.
5. Water daily or as needed, depending on rain.
6. Enjoy your vegetables and the delicious herbs.

Why do it:
Planting certain herbs beside certain vegetables can help in many ways. Basil improves the flavor of the tomatoes. The basil can also keep away flies and mosquitoes. Chives can improve the flavor and growth of the carrots. By planting the oregano beside the cucumber, it helps keep the cucumber beetles away.

Notes for the Activity:

Nature Journal

What you'll need:
1. A place outside to plant a garden.
2. Seeds or plants of tomatoes, basil, chives, carrots, cucumbers, and oregano.

How to do it:
1. Prepare your garden for planting.
2. Plant the tomatoes beside the basil.
3. Plant the chives beside the carrots.
4. Plant the cucumbers beside the oregano.
5. Water daily or as needed, depending on rain.
6. Enjoy your vegetables and the delicious herbs.

Why do it:
Planting certain herbs beside certain vegetables can help in many ways. Basil improves the flavor of the tomatoes. The basil can also keep away flies and mosquitoes. Chives can improve the flavor and growth of the carrots. By planting the oregano beside the cucumber, it helps keep the cucumber beetles away.

Notes for the Activity:

Nature Journal

What you'll need:
1. Computer paper that has been used only on one side.
2. Two rubber bands
3. A stick
4. Markers/crayons

How to do it:
1. Cut the paper to the desired size of the nature journal.
2. Poke two holes on the sides
3. Cut the rubber band in half and put it through the hole and tie it together. Repeat for the other hole.
4. Slide the stick under each rubber band.
5. Decorate the front of the nature journal.
6. Walk around outside with the nature journal sketching things in nature.

Why do it:
By using computer or drawing paper that has been used on only one side, you are recycling the paper. Paper that would usually be thrown away is now being used. Watching nature is a great way to know the earth. When we show our children how beautiful nature is, it will hopefully make them want to keep it beautiful.

Notes for the Activity:

Recycling Poster/Recycling Boxes/Containers

What you'll need:
1. Poster board or a large piece of paper
2. Markers/crayons
3. Three boxes or containers for recycling

How to do it:
1. Draw a poster explaining how and what can be recycled. Talk about plastic, glass, and cans.
2. Find a spot to put the three boxes or containers. Label each one as "glass," "plastic," and "cans."
3. Place the poster by the boxes/containers.
4. Recycle your glass, plastic, and cans in the appropriate box.

Why do it:
Remembering to recycle is very important. If a family is just starting to recycle, the poster by the recycling boxes/container is a good reminder.

Notes for the Activity:

Make a Light Chart

What you'll need:
1. Poster Board or a large piece of paper.
2. Markers/crayons
3. Small stickers

How to do it:
1. Make a chart with everyone's name on it. Make space to put stickers every time that person remembers to turn out the light when leaving a room.
2. The person with the most stickers at the end of the week gets to pick a game (board game, outside game) for the family to play.
3. If someone forgets to turn off a light and someone else turns it off, the person who turned it off gets the sticker.

Why do it
Remembering to turn off the lights when you leave a room saves energy and money. A simple chart like this gives children and adults a reminder. At the end of the week, it is fun to pick a game for family time together.

Notes for the Activity:

Clean Sinks

What You'll Need:
1. A bottle of vinegar
2. A box of baking soda

How to Do It:
1. Go around to all the sinks in your home and let your child put some baking soda in the sink drain and then let them pour vinegar down the drain.

Why to Do It:
Using vinegar and baking soda is a natural way to clean and disinfect your sinks. The chemical reaction is safe and fun for children to watch. Many sink cleaners can contain toxic ingredients and they can let off a toxic smell. This method of cleaning your sink is completely safe for you and your child.

Notes for the Activity:

Craft Time

What You'll Need:
1. Look in your "junk drawers," craft supplies and counter tops for any items that you would normally throw away.
2. Glue, paper, markers/crayons

How to Do It:
1. Use the collected items to create a cool craft. It can be anything from a necklace to a paperweight. Use your imagination and have fun.

Why to Do It:
You are recycling old, useless materials instead of throwing them away.

Notes for the Activity:

Bubble Blower

What You'll Need:
2. Empty, cleaned 2 liter bottle of soda.
3. Cut the bottle in half. Keep the top half. Save the bottom for the next activity (Container Garden #2)
4. Bubble solution
5. Container to pour the bubble solution into.

How to Do It:
1. Pour the bubble solution into a shallow container.
2. Dip the half bottle in the bubble solution and gently blow through the top of the bottle.

Why to Do It:
You are recycling a plastic product by turning it into something else. Children love bubbles and this is a fun family activity.

Notes for the Activity:

Container Garden #2

What you'll need:
1. The bottom half of the plastic 2 liter soda bottle from the previous activity
2. Potting soil/compost
3. Seeds or plants
4. Small rocks

How to Do It:
1. Put a few small rocks in the bottom of the plastic container.
2. Add potting soil and compost.
3. Plant seeds or plants.
4. Water often.

Why to Do It:
In the Bubble Blower activity you only used the top half of the bottle. In this activity, you can use the rest of the bottle. It makes a great container garden. You are recycling an item that would usually be thrown away. Your child will get the chance to see roots growing from the plants because the plastic bottle is translucent.

Notes for the Activity:

Bird Feeder

What You'll Need:
1. An empty, cleaned gallon milk jug
2. Wire (for hanging)
3. Small stick
4. Birdseed

How to Do It:
1. Cut a scoop shape out of the milk jug. Be sure to keep the bottom a few inches tall because it will hold the bird seed. The final shape should resemble an "L."
2. Poke two holes in the plastic at the top. Thread the wire through the holes for hanging.
3. Poke two small holes (one in the back and one in the front). Push the stick through the holes. This will be where the bird stands.
4. Fill the jug with birdseed.
5. Hang it on a tree.

Why to Do It:
You are recycling a milk jug into a bird feeder. You are helping the environment by reducing trash and feeding the birds. Children and adults enjoy watching birds.

Notes for the Activity:

Farmer's Market

What You'll Need:
1. A local farmer's market
2. Fabric shopping bag

How to Do It:
1. Take your child to a farmer's market. Ask questions about the produce. Encourage your child to ask questions too.
2. Buy some produce to use in a meal.

Why to Do It
Buying organic produce from a farmer's market is a great way to become green. Talking to the farmers is a way to learn more about organic farming.

Notes for the Activity:

Washing Dishes the Green Way

What you'll need:
1. Two sinks filled with water in the kitchen. (If you don't have two sinks, you can fill one sink and use a dish pan for the other sink.) Use the drain plugs to keep the water in. Add soap to one sink.
2. Dirty dishes

How to Do It:
1. Have your child help you wash the dishes. Use one sink for washing and the other for rinsing.

Why to Do It:
Water is wasted when it continually runs while people wash dishes. By using two sinks with water, it saves water. This also uses less water than a dishwasher.

Notes for the Activity:

Donate Craft Items

What You'll Need:
1. Old craft supplies (pom poms, sequins, craft foam, cotton balls, etc.)

How to Do It:
1. Gather craft or recyclable items that could be used as craft materials.
2. Donate the items to schools or daycares.

Why to Do It:
Schools and daycares use a variety of materials for crafts. You are donating or recycling your old items so that someone else can turn them into something new.

Notes for the Activity:

Have a Green Picnic

What you'll need:
1. Organic food
2. Real plates, cups, and silverware (not paper or plastic)

How to Do It:
1. Pick a nice shady spot for a green picnic. Try to eat as organic as possible. Try not to create a lot of waste or cause pollution.
2. If you do use items that can be recycled, be sure to put them into a recycling box.

Why to Do It:
Picnics are a nice way to enjoy nature and the environment. By having a green picnic you can be friendly to the Earth while enjoying it.

Notes for the Activity:

Make Scratch Paper

What You'll Need:
1. Computer paper or drawing paper that has only been used on one side
2. Scissors
3. Small basket

How to Do It:
1. Decide on a size for your scrap paper and then cut each paper that size.
2. Depending on the age of your child, he/she can use children's scissors and help to cut the paper.
3. Put the scrap paper into the basket.
4. Use the scrap paper anytime you need to write a note.

Why to Do It:
Most people throw away paper after only using one side. By using both sides of the paper, you are recycling.

Notes for the Activity:

Adopt Something

What you'll Need:
1. An animal, a stream, a whale, or an environment cause to adopt.

How to Do It:
1. Research on the Internet or your local library to find something to adopt. This could be an actual animal that you take home from the humane shelter or an animal you can sponsor. Sometimes you can find rivers, streams, or an environmental cause that needs sponsors too.

Why to Do It:
There are many animals and environmental causes that need our help. By adopting or sponsoring we are doing our part to contribute to the balance of our environment.

Notes for the Activity:

Clean Up Time

What You'll Need:
2. A location to clean up (a park, stream, or creek)
3. Gardening gloves
4. Gardening tools
5. Bags (to collect trash)
6. Plants (businesses may donate)

How to Do It:
1. Once you have picked an area, clean up the area.
2. Collect any trash in the area.
3. Pull weeds
4. Plant the plants

Why to Do It:
Cleaning up an area is a way to do your part in helping the environment. Cleaning up areas makes them look nicer and creates new environments for children and animals to play in.

Notes for the Activity:

Indoor Golf Game

What You'll Need:
1. Empty and cleaned juice cartons cut in half
2. Small ball
3. Pretend golf club or stick

How to Do It:
1. Use the cut cartons as the different "golf holes."
2. Set up the cut cartons in a room.
3. Take turns trying to hit the ball into each carton.

Why to Do It:
By using the old juice cartons you are recycling a product that is usually thrown away. You are turning waste into a fun game. This cuts down on waste in landfills.

Notes for the Activity:

Vocabulary

Words to Teach Your Child

Acid rain - rain that has higher acidity because of environmental factors.

Biosphere - the part of the world that life can exist.

Bottles - a container that is usually glass or plastic that can hold liquids.

Cans - a container that is metal and shaped like a cylinder. Food and soda comes in cans.

Cardboard - a material similar to paper but much thicker that is used to make boxes.

CFC's - (chlorofluorocarbon) a compound used to help keep items cold. It causes ozone loss.

Clean - pollution- and dirt-free.

Climate change - a long-term change in a region's weather.

Compost - a mixture of decayed matter (leaves, rinds, organic material) that is used to help fertilize gardens and flowers.

Coral bleaching - the loss of color in coral due to environmental conditions.

Earth - the planet that we live on.

Ecology - the relationship between living things and their environment.

Efficient energy use - using less energy to perform the same service.

Energy - usable power such as heat and electricity.

Environment - your surroundings.

Environmental movement - changing our ways and becoming green.

Extinction - when a living species is no longer alive.

Fossil fuels - found in the top layer of the Earth.

Garbage - waste left over from food and food containers.

Garden - a place on the ground where vegetables, fruits, herbs, and flowers are grown.

Green - a term that refers to people making better choices for the environment and themselves.

Habitat - a place where animals or plants naturally live.

Habitat fragmentation - habitats changing due to natural processes or due to people clearing out areas.

Land pollution - contamination of the land and soil.

Landfill - a place where garbage and trash is buried under the ground in layers.

Light pollution - when too much light is used by people. This excessive light interferes with the natural way plants and animals live together.

Lights - something that helps us see.

Litter - trash that is not properly disposed of on the Earth.

Logging - when trees are cut down for lumber.

Natural - a product of nature.

Natural environment - all living and nonliving things that are naturally on Earth.

Newspaper - paper that is printed on and distributed daily. It contains news, articles, and pictures.

Ocean - large body of saltwater that covers almost three fourths of the Earth.

Ocean dumping - dumping wastes into certain parts of the ocean.

Oil spills - oil wastes that enter the ocean.

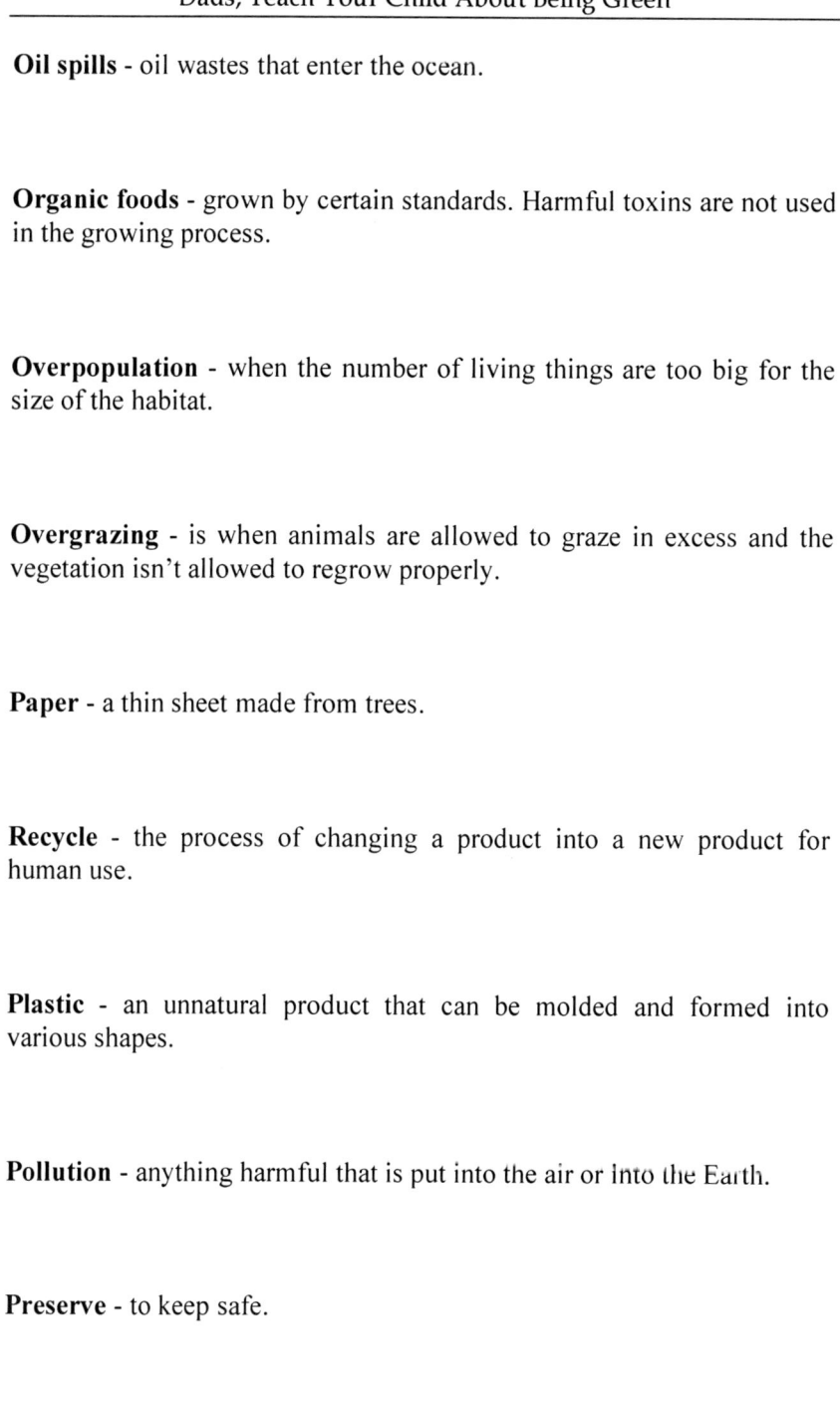

Organic foods - grown by certain standards. Harmful toxins are not used in the growing process.

Overpopulation - when the number of living things are too big for the size of the habitat.

Overgrazing - is when animals are allowed to graze in excess and the vegetation isn't allowed to regrow properly.

Paper - a thin sheet made from trees.

Recycle - the process of changing a product into a new product for human use.

Plastic - an unnatural product that can be molded and formed into various shapes.

Pollution - anything harmful that is put into the air or into the Earth.

Preserve - to keep safe.

Renew - to make something new again.

Renewable Energy - natural resources including sunlight, wind, and rain.

Sea level rise - an increase in sea level.

Soil - material of the Earth that plants can grow in.

Soil contamination - when man-made chemicals filter into the soil.

Soil erosion - the movement and change in land and soil due to environmental factors.

Solar energy - energy from the sun.

Toxic waste - chemicals in waste form that can be harmful to living things.

Trash - anything that has no use anymore and cannot be reused.

Tree - a plant with bark and leaves that can live for many years. Trees give us oxygen to breath.

Urban Sprawl - refers to cities growing into rural areas.

Volunteer - a person that does a job without getting paid.

Waste - any material that is left over and is not being used.

Wasteful - not using materials in an efficient manner.

Water - liquid that comes from the clouds.

Water crisis - refers the availability of water

Water cycle - the constant movement of our water.

Wood - a hard substance that comes from trees.

Worms - a soft bodied animal that crawls under the ground. They are very important composters.

Web Sites

http://www.itshouldbeeasybeinggreen.com/
This site has articles and blogs on being green. Categories include clothing, computers, health, energy, and food.

http://www.thegreenguide.com/
This site is an online magazine that helps families who are going green. Product reviews let you know if your current products are green. There are also buying guides, quizzes and helpful tips.

http://www.recycleworks.org/schools/educate.html
This site offers resources, curriculum, and project ideas for the classroom. However, any project or idea can be used at home.

http://www.epa.gov/kids/index.htm
This site is from the Environmental Protection Agency. There are resources to help families go green as well as fun environmental online games to play.

http://recycling.stanford.edu/facstaff/kids.html
This site, from Stanford University, is full of environmental websites for kids.

http://www.ivillage.com/green/family/0,,bmbzlqpb,00.html
This site is full of ways to teach kids how to go green. The information is broken down into age groups. There are ideas for helping the entire family go green.

http://www.nrdc.org/reference/kids.asp
This site, from the Natural Resource Defense Council, offers many resources for children and adults. It covers all areas of protecting the environment.

http://www.epa.state.il.us/education.html
This site, from the Illinois Environmental Protection Agency, offers many links for adults, and children. It explains why protecting the environment is important using online games and resources.

http://www.healthychild.org/
This site helps parents create a healthy, green home for babies and children. It includes resources, articles, and blogs.

http://www.localharvest.org/
This site helps people find the best organic food that is grown closest to them. It also helps them find online organic stores, farmer's markets, restaurants, and grocery stores.

http://www.compostguide.com/
This detailed site teaches about composting, including composting with worms. It tells what one can and can't compost and even has troubleshooting advice.

Class Notes

Fill in the Blanks Below

Name of Your Child:

Date You Started the Class:

What did your child do the best throughout the WonderDads class?

What activity did your child enjoy the most during the class?

What was the funniest thing your child did during a class?

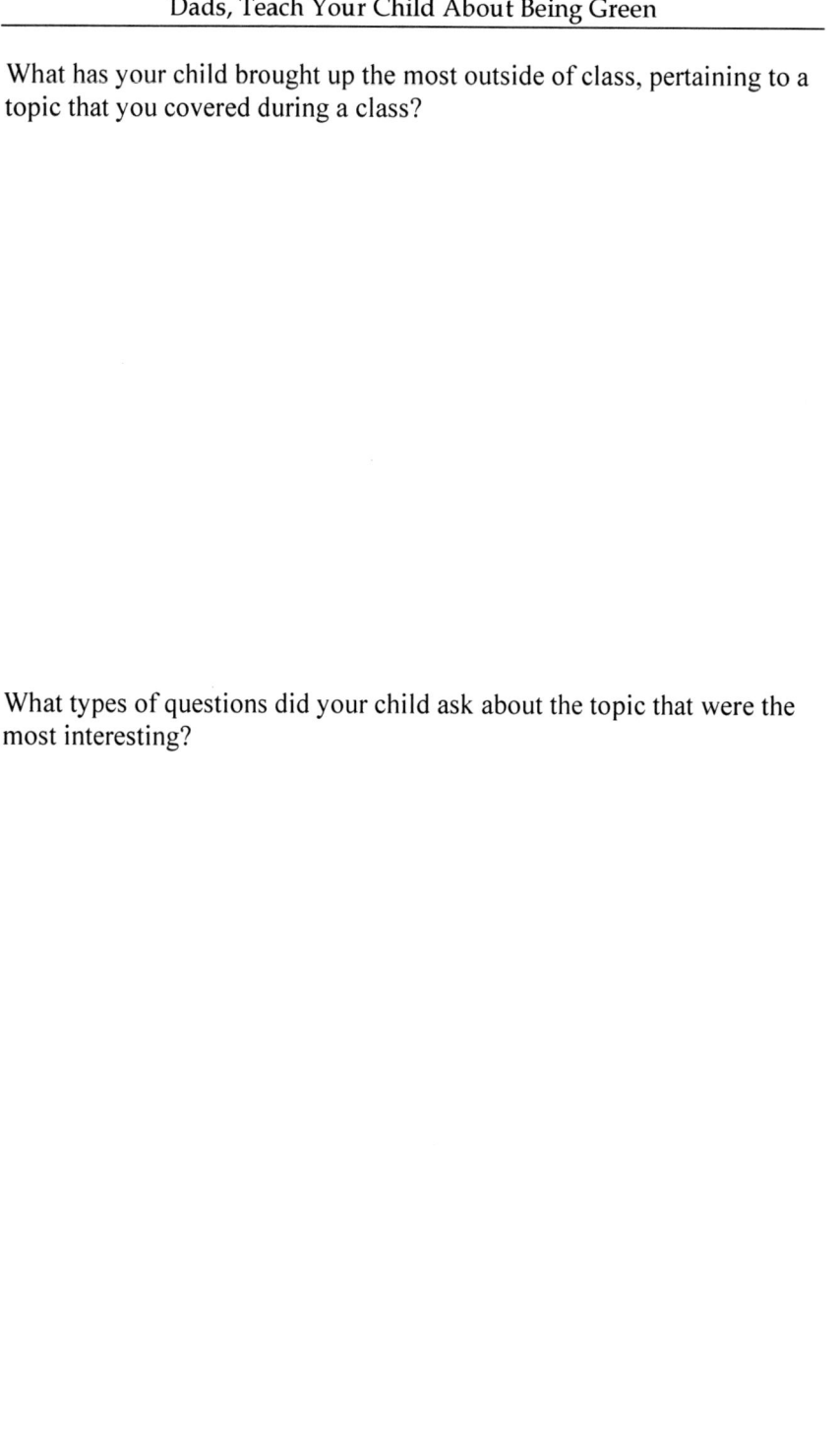

What has your child brought up the most outside of class, pertaining to a topic that you covered during a class?

What types of questions did your child ask about the topic that were the most interesting?

What surprised you the most about your child during the class?

What did you enjoy most about doing this WonderDads class with your child?

Letter to Your Child

Write the Letter in the Next 4 Pages

Write a letter to your child for them to read twenty years from now. Share your experiences taking this WonderDads class and why it was important to you that they learn about this topic. The letter will be enjoyable reading for them (and you) as the years pass.

Dads, Teach Your Child About Being Green

Keepsakes

Tape in Items Below

Tape in any photos, pictures, or other items that can be used as a keepsake to look back on teaching your child this class.

Dads, Teach Your Child About Being Green

The Dad's Activity Bag

Perfect for Books, Toys, Work Papers or Even Diapers

Extra-Long Shoulder Strap Makes it Easier to Carry Than Mom's Bags!

Navy Blue/Tan - $24.95

www.WonderDads.com/dadtote.asp

Dad's Hats

Tan Hat, Color Logo (Blue, Red, Yellow)

$24.95 + S&H

www.WonderDads.com/Merchandise4.asp

Kid's T-Shirts

Light Blue T-Shirt, Color Logo, Sizes – 2T, 3T, 4T

$19.95 + S&H

www.WonderDads.com/Merchandise1.asp

WonderDads Gift Packs

For Dads

Includes any book, a WonderDads baseball hat and a Dad's Tote Bag. A Savings of $10!

Only $49.95 + S&H

For Kids

Includes any book, a kid's t-shirt, a certificate of completion (for hanging on the child's wall) and a special gift-wrapped item (for the child when he/she finishes the class). A Savings of $20.

Only $39.95 + S&H

www.WonderDads.com

About the Author – Bobbi Ireland is a Freelance Children's Writer and Special Education Teacher from Robinson, Illinois.

She enjoys all of her spare time with her husband John, and their sons, Cameron and Preston.

Acknowledgements - A special thanks to Tricia for all of her help on becoming green and for testing out this book. She is the greenest person I know!

www.WonderDads.com

Printed in the United States
204415BV00005B/79-99/P